Sam and
Friends

The Barkers Club

This Sam and Friends Book,
"A Sister for Sam," belongs to:

_____

A Sister for Sam

A "Sam and Friends Book"

Written by **Vicki Diane Westling**

Illustrated by **Dan Drewes**

Chief Literary Critic **Michael Blue**

AuthorHouse™
1663 Liberty Drive
Bloomington, IN 47403
www.authorhouse.com
Phone: 1-800-839-8640

First published by AuthorHouse 9/28/2010

ISBN: 978-1-4520-7641-6 (sc)

Library of Congress Control Number: 2010913245

Printed in the United States of America

This book is printed on acid-free paper.

This Sam and Friends Book is dedicated to all children, but especially to those who are members of a blended family.

To my dog, Sam for constant inspiration and companionship, and to my husband Richard for his unwavering support and encouragement.

And, of course, to Cate! A beautiful black lab belonging to my very special Chief Literary Critic, Michael Blue.

A Sister for Sam

Sam had gone to bed for the night when he heard his mommy and daddy talking about getting another dog.

"Oh Boy, oh boy, oh boy," Sam whispered to himself in his softest woof possible. He wiggled and he turned, he got out of his bed and played with his tennis balls, he jumped on top of his mommy's bed and nuzzled her beneath her chin and licked her face. He was so happy.

The next morning, Sam awoke before sunrise and hurried over to the clubhouse. He was more excited than he had ever been, and he had to tell his friends the good news. He thought they would never come out.

Finally, he heard Rudie come out of his house. "It's about time you woke up, Rudie. I have been waiting for you," barked Sam.

"Good grief, Sam, you scared me half to death, what are you doing up so early. And, why are you in the clubhouse already?" growled Rudie.

"I have the best news in the whole wide world. Mommy and Daddy are getting another dog. Do you know what that means? I'm going to have a new little brother. Isn't that wonderful?" barked Sam. Then he did a flip and ran around chasing his tail.

"That might not be the best news, Sam. After all, you might not like having a brother. That would mean you would have to share your toys, you won't be the only dog in the house, and what could be worse, you could get a sister!" groaned Rudie.

"Blecch! Yikes! A sister. They have fleas," barked Sam. "Mommy would never do that to me. She loves me."

Boots entered the yard and came to where his friends were talking. "Hey what's going on?" he drawled.

"Mommy and Daddy are going to get another dog, and it might be a, yukky sister!" whined Sam.

"Now, Sam, it might be a brother, too," woofed Rudie, trying to make his little friend feel better.

"Sisters aren't so bad anyway, Sam," Boots barked, trying to reassure Sam. "I knew a girl dog once and she was kind of neat. She could run as fast as I could and she did all kinds of neat tricks. She could even catch a Frisbee." Boots gave Rudie a stern look for upsetting Sam.

"Yeah, Sam, Boots is right, it probably will be a brother dog, and even if it isn't, a sister dog won't be so bad. Its not like you'll have to play with her or anything," woofed Rudie as he put his paw on Sam's shoulder. "Come on, let's go down to the lake and chase the seagulls."

The three friends walked down to the lake. Sam was too depressed to run. He couldn't help but to think that his worse nightmare might come true and he would end up with a sister.

Once the seagulls saw the dogs coming toward them they knew something had to be wrong. The dogs were not running and jumping like they usually did and the birds didn't quite know what to make of it. "Better go get Hannibal," screeched one of the older seagulls to a younger one. "Fly fast, something is seriously wrong." The young seagull took off to find Hannibal while the other seagulls circled and flew up to the treetops where they perched and watched the three friends.

It took a while for the younger seagull to find Hannibal, but when he saw the tall grass moving in a straight line in old Farmer Campbell's field he knew it must be Hannibal. He swooped down and landed right in front of Hannibal's nose.

"What the heck," roared Hannibal "just what do you think you are doing you stupid seagull? You know I can eat birds for breakfast just as easily as I can eat mice." Then he put out his paws and roared as loudly as he could. The seagull did not budge. Hannibal roared again, and shook his paws toward the seagull. The seagull did not move. "Okay, what is it? There must be some reason that you are here, so what do you want?" demanded Hannibal.

"Come to the lake, quickly, there is something wrong with the dogs," chirped the little seagull.

Hannibal took off toward the lake at full speed. When he arrived at the shoreline he saw that the dogs were sitting together with their heads down.

"What's happening, boys?" meowed Hannibal in the most cheerful voice he could meow.

"I'm getting a sister," whined Sam.

"Oh, no, that is bad news," Hannibal meowed. "A girl! Yuk!"

Sam stood and turned to his friends, "I'm going home," he groaned as he walked slowly back to his house.

"I'm going to run away," he whimpered as he walked past the others.

Once back home, he went inside and found his favorite toy bear and a tennis ball. He went to his treat dish and took out three milk bone treats; he then put all of these things on his little soft blanket and dragged them out the door and over to the clubhouse.

"I'll stay here until I decide where to go," he mumbled to himself. But he was very tired. He lay down on his blanket and went to sleep.

"S-a-a-a-m. S-a-a-am," Sam's mommy called.

Sam didn't want to go home. He knew there would be a new dog in the house and it would probably be a sister. He didn't want to share his stuff, and he sure didn't want to share it with a girl, but his mommy kept calling and he knew he had to go home.

"Look, Sam, this is your new sister. Her name is Cate. Isn't she beautiful?" asked his mommy while she was rubbing his head.

He wished she wouldn't do that right now, he wanted to stay mad! Cate didn't look anything like him, and besides he wanted a brother. He shook his head and twitched his ears.

"Sam, not all brothers and sisters look alike," explained his mommy. "We are what is called a blended family. That means that we are not all the same color, age, boy or girl, we are each different but wonderful in our own way, do you understand?" mommy asked. She was still rubbing his head and behind his ears.

He tried to ignore her and Cate, but he couldn't. Cate was wonderful. She was a beautiful black lab. She wagged her tail, and she touched his nose with hers, she sniffed and woofed, and she really acted like she liked him. And he wanted to like her back, but she was a girl!

He promised himself that he wasn't going to like her. He put his nose in the air, dropped his tail straight down, and pulled his ears back. He walked away from her and went into his mommy's bedroom and got on the bed.

Cate followed him.

Sam jumped down from the bed and crawled behind the chair next to the window.

Cate followed him.

Finally he walked out of the house and ran to the clubhouse.

Cate followed him.

"Get out of our clubhouse, you are not wanted here. This is for me and my friends and we're all boys," growled Sam.

Cate didn't know what to do. Tears filled her eyes and she hung her head. As she started walking out of the clubhouse Boots, Rudie and Hannibal came running toward her barking and meowing for all they were worth.

Cate was startled and she yelped and hid behind Sam, after all he was her brother and she needed to be protected.

"Hey, you guys, you didn't have to scare her, can't you act like gentlemen?" barked Sam.

"Who is she?" woofed Boots

"This is my new sister, her name is Cate," barked Sam.

"Hi, I'm Hannibal," purred Hannibal as he put out his paw toward Cate.

"And, my name is Rudie," woofed Rudie.

"Good to meet you, Cate, my name is Boots," Boots groaned lazily.

"Hi. I'm Cate. I'm Sam's new sister," woofed Cate.

"Well, what do you think, guys? How do you like my new sister? Should we let her stay?" Sam barked.

"Its okay with me if it's okay with you, Sam," Boots barked.

"Yeah, I'm good with it," woofed Rudie.

"Count me in, too," meowed Hannibal.

"Okay, then, its official. Cate, welcome to 'The Barkers' you're our first girl," barked Sam as he gave his new sister a hug.

"Now, wait a minute, Sam. One girl is enough!" purred Hannibal, "unless of course it's a mouse."

Character Lesson: Family: A family doesn't have to have two people, or ten. It is just people who love each other and who live together. Sometimes a family has a mommy and a daddy and some boys and some girls, and sometimes it means just a mommy or just a daddy, or even two mommies or two daddies. Sometimes there is no mommy or daddy and the children live with an aunt, an uncle or grandparent. Family members are not always the same color, and they don't always look alike. Family doesn't always mean blood relatives, it just means acceptance, love and caring for each other.

A Barker is always honest, fair, trustworthy and respectful of others.

Join The Barkers at www.vickiwestling.com

Email Sam and his friends at sam_and_friends@yahoo.com

Write to Sam and his friends at:

Sam and Friends
130 South Ocelot Street
Dunkirk, NY 14048

www.ingramcontent.com/pod-product-compliance
Lightning Source LLC
Chambersburg PA
CBHW060808290526
45792CB00005BA/1572

9781452076416